THE SEVEN DI

A Step-By-Step Journey to Awakening the Heart

THE SEVEN DESTINIES OF LOVE

A Step-By-Step Journey to Awakening the Heart

Claudia de Llano

Cherish
EDITIONS

First published in Great Britain 2023 by Cherish Editions

Cherish Editions is a trading style of Shaw Callaghan Ltd & Shaw Callaghan 23 USA, INC.

The Foundation Centre

Navigation House, 48 Millgate, Newark

Nottinghamshire NG24 4TS UK

www.triggerhub.org

British Library Cataloguing in Publication Data

A CIP catalogue record for this book is available upon request from the British Library

ISBN: 978-1-913615-82-6

This book is also available in the following eBook formats:

ePUB: 978-1-913615-83-3

Cover design by More Visual

Typeset by Lapiz Digital Services

Cover illustration by Renny Ruiz

CONTENTS

Foreword   1

Chapter 1: Soul Love – The First Destiny   5
Chapter 2: Embodied Love – The Second Destiny   15
Chapter 3: Connected Love – The Third Destiny   21
Chapter 4: Ancestral Love – The Fourth Destiny   29
Chapter 5: Spiritual Love – The Fifth Destiny   35
Chapter 6: Awakening Love – The Sixth Destiny   45
Chapter 7: Amaranthine Love – The Seventh Destiny   55

Conclusion   59

The Seven Destinies of Love Quiz   61
Your Love Destiny Journal   77

Endorsements   93
About the Author   95
Acknowledgements   97

To all that is divine: the earth, the cosmos, the lineage of ancestry that came before us and those that will come after us, Ho'oponopono.

In loving memory of Steven Ma, John Jung and Yaphet Kotto.

FOREWORD

I believe I was born in joy. In the depths of my being, this I remember. Throughout my years of teaching and providing therapy, I am certain students and clients have all come to remember. They come to remember joy, the road to self, the road to love. We are entrenched in cultural sorrow, where the focus of our stories is filled with pain, loss and struggle. My aim is to be a part of the exchange that moves our stories to a consciousness of love. This is my great love story. I hope this is where you come to remember and awaken to yours.

***

I remember the first time I met God. I was in a quaint little town in New Zealand settled somewhere back in the early 1900s. Just the day before, my husband had been asking me about my definition of God. I tried to explain that the spiritual literature referred to God as a consciousness within, not a punishing and rewarding entity floating in the skies and tallying up our actions like some grocery receipt. In this rather failed attempt at explaining what I had begun to experience as God, I referred to Ram Dass, whom I had never met but considered a lifetime mentor and guide. He said, "Treat everyone you meet like God in drag." So, there I was in this flawlessly manicured town that felt like a movie set: cars from the 1920s, an old train preserved to perfection, antique shops mixed with new import shops and tourists everywhere running to buy their wares. With Ram Dass' words at heart, the apparition of

God materialized in front of me with a five o'clock shadow, a blue miniskirt and a tie-dye shirt. And God was beautiful.

At the time, I was wrapped in my professional identity as a graduate school instructor with a specialization in multiculturalism, social justice and diversity – a champion of those oppressed by majority force. And yet there I was, thinking, "I didn't expect diversity to be represented in a small town," followed by the thought that my reaction was an erroneous assumption. And then I remembered Ram Dass' words and thought, "There is God. And the God that is in you is in me." The judgment suddenly fell away as I was silenced by that inner knowing that we are all the one. I returned to love.

I often come across people who are afraid to use the word "love" in professional and personal contexts because they feel it has been overused or is somehow too charged with multiple meanings or experiences. Words are never enough to describe something that simply is. Our subjective perceptions taint words as we try to capture human experience, and words slowly become an amalgamation of some collective consciousness that belongs to the time and place when that word began. I felt this way about the word "God".

My spiritual journey began early, through a myriad of different ceremonies and celebrations, as well as through visits to churches, synagogues and temples whenever I got invited by childhood friends and family. None of these experiences directly belonged to me. Early on, my father told me religious and spiritual beliefs are of a private nature and strictly belong to the individual. Therefore, he would never impose any particular belief system on me. He encouraged self-exploration and my choice to follow or not follow any particular dogma once of I was of age and personal agency. As a child, this boggled me, given that most people I knew had a doctrine with which they seemed to belong to or identify. As my spiritual awakening would come many years later, I had no idea the profound freedom my father's experience and wisdom would provide me. There is no more humbling or beautiful a journey than the one of awakening. It is painfully weary, full of tunnels, obstacles and shadows. There is also deep strength, resilience, bliss and peace. Above all, there is the interminable grind of integrating these pieces into our life's work until our hearts break, become whole, dissolve and return to the one.

Each journey is inspired and can be full of boundless potential to evolve as we come into the deep release of being in the bareness of love. Awakening through love allows one's entire state of being to transform with grace. Our perspective on life, meaning and direction begin to change as we find our internal home. Clarity and bliss become a state, emptiness becomes fullness, and at some point, you transition from seeking to trusting, trusting to knowing, and finally into unknowing. The divine that is in you is in me, and it is all love.

There are seven destinies of love we come to live and play out during our time here on earth. The first destiny is **soul love**, the love where we come to an agreement between our body, mind and spirit that, in whatever way we have come to this journey, there is a wisdom within us that, when cultivated and trusted, becomes the force so worthy of love, it can embrace and simultaneously let go. With this destiny, we can truly fall into and be love.

The second destiny is **embodied love.** This is the love of essentiality, an embodiment of the notion that all things are alive, but, in particular, our connection to nature and the elements of which we are comprised. This allows us to manifest a universe field of infinite dimension that is all at once whole.

The third destiny is **connected love**, an understanding of our mental, physical and emotional connection to familial, romantic and social relationships. These bonds elevate our life lessons by the way we show up for those we love.

The fourth destiny is **ancestral love**. This is a love of timelessness, where we recognize that our imprints – past, present and future – are connected to our existence right now. Integrating our ancestry tallies the contribution of our human journey, thus creating an infinite legacy. This legacy becomes our way of breathing, loving and perceiving life in boundless presence.

The fifth destiny is **spiritual love.** This love is our connection to the universe, the cosmos and the ethereal worlds. This love lets go of linear thinking and allows the possibility of an expanded realization that goes beyond the five senses. Through this love, we can release judgement and truly elevate our consciousness.

The sixth destiny is the **awakening love** This is a conscious spiritual journey of self-realization: actualization of the voice of the heart. In this love, we find forgiveness; that is, a letting-go of emotions that were meant to be lessons, not chains. Through the teachings of these feelings, a creation and realization of who we really are begins to emerge and transport us into realms outside of ourselves.

The seventh destiny is **amaranthine love** – the realization that our essence is immutable, our imprint is infinite, and our love is unending. We let go of everything else so that we may step into dissolution, true freedom – the ultimate love.

These destinies encompass the human spiritual journey of love. Hopefully through this process we can also learn something about how to love, too. Our love destinies are not always linear. We move in and out of them, sometimes bypassing them altogether or only working through parts of them. The key is that when we become aware of them, we have a context for how we wish to develop and connect to our own meaning and experience of love. Your definitions of these categories lie above what you read here. At the beginning and end of it all, there only is one love, and it is you. Create your own destiny, for it is in your energy field to do so.

CHAPTER 1

SOUL LOVE – THE FIRST DESTINY

What if peace wanted to stay in the orbit of your heart
*   where it has never left?*
What if peace wanted to stay in the vastness of your
*   mind where the kaleidoscope of chaos is dreamt?*
What if peace wanted to stay in the tremble of your
*   hands where hope is felt?*
What if peace wanted to stay in the rhythm of your chest
*   where the chant of your breath is life itself?*
What if peace wanted to stay in the roots of your heels
*   where connection is a primal mystic?*
What if peace wanted to stay in your throat, where fires
*   of revelation burn with compassion?*
What if peace wanted to stay in your soul, in your
*   essence, in your being, in your light, in your energy,*
*   in your journey, in your emptiness, in your void,*
*   where love is all there is?*

There is nothing wrong with allowing our house to be built of peace. Our internal home is where love begins. Love is lost and found in the dichotomous experience of the human system. As newborns, non-verbal perception and communication flood our days while we become attuned to sounds, physical contact, feeding, seeing, touching. How different this must be from the internal symphony of the womb, where the mechanics of the organs, fluids and ever-transmuting cells sing in their state of creation. In this sea of the body, we are naturally born into the rhythmic experience of simultaneous motion and stillness all at once. This is peace. It's knowing that the perpetual motion of life and matter are ceaseless, and the acceptance of this flow is our tranquillity. Only in this tranquillity can we truly stay connected to the love within, because here in this beginning, you are not told who to be, you simply are. And what you are is love.

Somewhere along the way, we lose this connection, yet the prescription is as simple as it always was: listen, sit and be just as you are. Somehow, we've created a world that encourages fragmentation and robs us of what matters most to our hearts: an internal quietude where we are so deeply connected to the vibration of life that we can tune into its hum and return to that grounding state where everything is capable of wellness and pure being. We've gone from productivity to a level of consumerism so unachievable that we have truly created an internal war where the soul cannot find its place. It is here that our identification with our minds – and hence our thoughts – begins to filter and thereby distorts who we think we are. Who we think we are, our self-identity, becomes a collection of achievements, rather than a fluid experience of whole love. The notion that we are more than our thoughts is not a new concept, but in modern cultures, the cultivation of our soul beyond the mind is not innate from childhood and therefore must be developed. We must create an environment that teaches us to respect our minds, our feelings, our gut, our heart and other internal senses that are informing us of what we need to reach this state.

Soul love is feeling critically. In Western culture, we deeply value the idea of critical thinking – that is, to use our discerning mind to analyse, criticize, construct and deconstruct our learning. In matters of soul love, it is important to learn to feel critically, or learn to discern our feelings and know when and how much to follow them. Our body is our guide. The body is a multifaceted instrument that is constantly informing us of its wants and needs and the true north of our physical being. Feelings are like thoughts: the more we indulge ourselves in learning to identify our feelings, the better equipped we are to cope with them. But feelings are more than a system for the mind to dominate or express. They are the human thermostat that not only keeps us connected to ourselves and others, but to the magnificence of our humanity. Our feelings are always there. Some feelings are more useful than others, and learning to feel critically matters to their function in our ultimate connection to the human experience. Whether we feel numbness, suffering, elation or bliss, each one is a path to our humanity. How extraordinary to have such a measurement to tell us that we are on track with our soul's path or that indeed we need to redirect. Learning to feel critically means taking the action to explore such feelings and discover the language of your feelings. It means knowing when to respond to feelings and when to let them be. It also means learning the trajectory where we come to recognize that emotions evolve, resolve and dissolve.

Acknowledging the idea that the universe is in perpetual motion means realizing that so too are our biosystems and, hence, our feelings. "I can't get rid of this feeling" is a thought about an immobile state. Feeling critically, on the other hand, is noticing the thought that accompanies the feeling and nurturing that feeling into movement. Movement only happens when we learn to recognize the feeling as a sign, acknowledge it and begin to nurture it with our own love. Admittedly, it's hard to love our pain. Learning to love ourselves is a mission in itself. But in so doing, by learning to love our pain, we begin to love all the parts of ourselves into wholeness. To be clear, I realize that, for some, this may sound like ambiguous or even dangerous territory. I don't want to create the misunderstanding that to love our pain means to necessarily love what you or someone else did. It means to love the feelings that arose to inform your heart of the choice to shut down or to awaken. It means that if you were hurt in some way, you can reconnect with that version of yourself at that point in time and begin to love those feelings through your internal relationship with your soul today. It means reconnecting to that state of love you were meant to always have in your presence, even when you hurt. So, when you feel pain for children in the world who are suffering from hunger or abuse, it means you should go inside that part of yourself that feels the pain and say, "Thank you for the aliveness within me – this instrument of feeling that is my thermostat for connection to myself and others." Sometimes this feeling will be a call to action in your life; sometimes it will be a bridge to something else; and sometimes it will simply be a passing feeling and nothing more. But by acknowledging the feeling and attending to your relationship with it, the feeling can evolve.

When feelings are attended to with love, we can resolve them. Because we are in a constant flow, so are our feelings. Therefore, recognition, acknowledgement and attending to our feelings helps to resolve them. We do so not necessarily so we can fix these feelings, but so we can move through them. It is to say to one's heart, "I hear you, I see you, I hold space for you and love you through it all." On the other hand, not all feelings are meant to be resolved. Feelings are only one dimension of our human experience; therefore, they do not need to be front and centre of it all. They can simply be an aspect of your heart's curriculum. By treating our feelings as lessons, we can ask ourselves what each feeling is trying to teach us. And from this space of curiosity, we can show up for the heart's message rather than get hung up on feeling more of something. Only then can we begin to see that we are not our loss, our gain, our fear, our happiness, our anger or our anxiety. These feelings are markers on the pages of our book and there to aid the evolution of our human experience through the lessons they invoke.

Our feelings are not a static state of identity. To this end, our human experience is evolving. Even if we perceive our life to be one of little change, we are a part of a bigger system that is changing and so, therefore, are you. Moving through our feelings is the path to the expansion of our being. When we move through our feelings from mind to movement, we allow ourselves to enter a deeper connection beyond the self – and to expand the development of our humanity.

To expand our emotional development, we must create a relationship with our feelings. That relationship can be self-defined, but like all relationships, it requires some basics: nurture, validation, reflection, growth, shelter, sustenance, freedom to be and freedom to fly. Each feeling has a road whereby it either comes or goes, but the road leads to the same place. So, your relationship to your feelings will determine how functional that road is. There is a Sufi parable about Junaid, a well-known mystic. Junaid leads his disciples into the local town bazaar, where he and his followers encounter a man leading a cow by a rope. The mystic asks his followers who is bound to whom: the man to the cow or the cow to the man. The followers, seeing the obvious, state that the cow is the servant bound to his master. Just then, the mystic cuts the rope and the cow takes off. The man who leads the cow becomes angered to see the cow run away, untethered and free. The mystic asks his followers rhetorically, "Who is bound to whom?"

Like this parable, the relationship to our feelings is not always the one we believe it to be. Is it us who invested in a feeling, or is the feeling invested in us? The moment we loosen the grip on our feelings, they begin to fall away. But it is the nature of the mind to hold on. The heart does not hold on – the heart loves unconditionally. The heart holds the feeling with a warm embrace and says, "I hear you, I am here for you, and I will hold the space beyond your mind." So, allow your feelings to come and reach your shores, but also allow them to recede, fade and return to the sea of still waters and dissolve.

When we have resolved our relationship with our feelings, we can then allow them to dissolve. Only through this transformation do we step into the space of all that is everything and the everything that is nothing. In this process, our feelings transform into dynamic particles of light, undefined, free and limitless – pure soul essence of everything and nothing all at once. Letting go into the magnificence of the unknown and surrendering in the greatness of all existence means that we'll experience uninhibited, spontaneous co-creation and dissolution into love. Acknowledge, nurture and release your feelings into the abyss of love that lies within your heart.

Soul love is listening to our bodies and developing a soul language. When we learn to listen to our bodies, we develop a soul language of appreciation for the brilliance of our incarnation. Each internal pain, ache, strain, pleasure and relaxation rests within our physicality, begging us to listen and respond while revealing truths. The body is our learning centre. We can feel a sensation and even ask the sensation or the physicality what it is trying to tell us. The body will answer with what most of us might describe as intuition, or a gut reaction. Of course, we must be critical about this exchange. If the body says, "Eat chocolate," and we respond, we may not be aware that the body is seeking the composition or a particular element of chocolate and asking us to bring it in for its purpose – whether healing, pleasure or both. However, if the brain then says, "Yum, I want to do that again and again," without tuning into the body's true need and egoless feeling, the discernment is lost. In real life, this is evident when everything in our body tells us something isn't right: "Don't accept that job," or, "Don't move into that place," or, "Don't buy that." But survival kicks in and the mind rationalizes, telling us we really need the money or to just go for it for whatever reason. And then the outcome is a disappointment or lands us in a new struggle. When this happens, we get caught in a loop of outcomes that deplete our sense of happiness and well-being. These thoughts and chain reactions steal our energy and inner peace. They create new vibrations that make us feel ill. Similarly, we do this with relationships. We agree to pursue a relationship or say yes when we know our body says no. The mind appears once again with its learned rationalizations that usually justify another's being while ignoring our own. Now, this doesn't mean we do everything toward which our feelings push us. It is a critical process where we must first learn our internal language of soul love.

The language of soul love is manifested awareness. When the heart looks tenderly at a newborn or something equally as filling, our whole body smiles as we manifest a love awareness. When you are a child, this means something like, "I want to be a race car driver!" Then, our conscious reality kicks in through the years and says, "That's not safe, I can't afford it, it's not a sustainable career." So, when we understand the language of soul love, it's just like the feeling that the child experiences when their hands are on that wheel, and their foot is on the pedal, and the speed is power, freedom, fun and nothing but the present moment. *Ah...* and then we can read the body as it sits in a place of well-being because the body loves its own power, freedom, fun and presence. This awareness of feeling can then be used critically. Is it cars I want to race, and how can I get there? Or is it something else that creates those feelings of power, freedom, fun and presence, and what does that translate into? Then, we respond by applying those feelings to the real world, rather than writing them off and getting a job that creates the opposite of what we sought.

Of course, the real world is completely subjective. You have one mission here on earth: return to love. Create your own reality with love. By fully evolving into love, how you serve in your life becomes a transmission of what you radiate and shapes how everyone and everything around you responds. This will shape a new reality that is elevated by what you are meant to be.

Soul love is sanctuary. Despite all the times you felt insecure in your life, less than or perhaps not capable, it turns out that there is no such thing as superiority or inferiority. In the spirit of oneness, we are all equal. Only hatred and fear act as the great dividers of our oneness. Oneness does not mean we are all the same expressions of love, but that it is our combined expression of pure love that raises us into the frequency of soul love. Soul love is a sanctuary of cultivated, unconditional acceptance of someone in their full expression. We must be secure in ourselves, our experiences and our truths to feel this sanctuary. Let's suppose you prefer soft, neutral colours. And when you see this palate you think, "Now, that is beautiful." Then, when you see another palate of loud, bright colours, you judge this display with dislike – you cannot see its beauty. This is because you're trapped in a partial reality. This is the split human experience, wherein you can only see beauty through the lens of your bias. That's a partial picture because you are blinded from seeing another's expression in its entirety. Witnessing with curiosity and appreciation of another's vision and expression is the sanctuary of soul love. It's stepping into an environment you would have never chosen, and rather than reacting to it, you see it through feeling, ambience and spirit. This doesn't mean you have to like it, but it does mean you can appreciate the perspective from a place of soul love. The best example I can give of this happened when my family and I moved from the United States into a new home in the warm and lively climate of Sydney, Australia. My daughter was two years old at the time, and the world was still somewhat of a blank slate to her. She had little context for what our culture defines as good versus evil, love versus hate, or beautiful versus ugly. So, I'm looking down at the floor of our new house and I see a cockroach crossing the floor. Now, my reactive response is immediate. I'm in disgust of this creature. I feel threatened by this creature. I want to be rid of this creature. So instead, I look down at it and I show it to my daughter because I'm pretty sure she's never seen a cockroach before. And though I can't recall my exact words, I do clearly recall that she looked down at the creature and, with all the sincerity in her heart and a soft tone of love in her voice, said, "Mom, look at it; it's beautiful!" Her words stopped me in my tracks because I immediately wanted to tell her how it could carry disease and that she shouldn't touch it and that, in fact, it was not beautiful, but rather quite gross. And that's how we lose our soul language. Someone else tells us that the feelings about our experiences are false or wrong. In that moment, my daughter could see the beauty in the creature because she saw through an unfiltered lens of unconditioned bias. She had no attachment to what I had been taught that then shaped my response. She saw a soul.

Soul love is seeing from soul to soul. How do we teach ourselves to see a soul from the soul? How do we release the indoctrination of intellect that blocks intuition and multisensory perception from our experience of the world? Whatever the means, it's our stepping away from the judgement of the "right" method that turns us inward toward deep listening. It is up to us to find and cultivate this space according to our own criticism and not those prescribed by cultural trends. This is soul love, the ability to hear your own voice and attend to it lovingly. Creating or recreating a life that makes room for this space is needed. Otherwise, we are trapped in the noise of everyday life that numbs us, taps us out and prevents us from checking back in.

One of the ways we can learn to see ourselves is by creating a listening relationship between the mind and body, where acknowledgement, nurturing, forgiveness and non-judgement are part of the relationship. Try to feel the ache in your heart or your ankle or wherever it may be without the need to judge it, question it, blame someone, fix it or panic. Feel, notice, allow and then ask the mind to engage with it in a nurturing, attentive, non-judgemental way. Listen to the message of the feeling and then simply allow it to dissolve into awareness. What happens when you have the option to either have awareness of the feeling or pay sole attention to the feeling? Listening expands the ability to hear the inner instrument of your instinct and lets your awareness be. In this process, answers naturally arise. There are great lessons here for us all. Listening is not a means to an end, whereby you say something, another then responds, and we somehow communicate understanding. Listening is tuning into the very vibration of experience without knowing, understanding or rationalizing. Listening is more than the auditory process. It is the process that lends itself to feeling. And that feeling can be used as information. We either respond to the feeling or we simply allow it. We all want to be heard. And when we learn to hear ourselves, only then can we be seen. When we learn to listen to ourselves, only then can we truly enter the silence that listens to another with absolute presence. When we are there wholly for our own soul and learn to be there wholly for another soul, our home becomes one of true peace.

CHAPTER 2

EMBODIED LOVE –
THE SECOND DESTINY

The Balinese banyan tree stood there,
With stories to tell.
Root by root,
it reached toward the earth,
Each connection building a memoir.
Branch by branch,
It reached toward the skies,
And through the darkness of its dense, deep green,
I could no longer see.
But its shadows lulled me,
Into that deep silence,
That hums the song of the universe,
And then I fell into the sound of the waves
Crawling toward the seashore,
And felt the birds rustling in the trees
Until every part of my being,
Electrified with centripetal motion
Became my peace.

Love of being is the love of essentiality, a love that is absolute, indispensable and necessary because it is the love of life, of being alive. This love lends itself to the notion that all things animate and inanimate are flourishing as a part of the vibrational source of life, of which we are an inseparable part. This inseparability of being demands our connection to all living things and extends our love of nature and connection to the elements, which are necessary relationships. Through them, we can make a full expression of the love within us, and that allows us to manifest a universe filled with capability, prospect and growth. Alan Watts, the 20th century philosopher, taught us that we are not separate from nature – we are a part of nature. But we grow up thinking we are either city or country, and that it's somehow a choice. We are always in need of nature as much as nature needs us. We are undeniably a part of the ecosystem and in a relationship with it, however functional or dysfunctional. We are one more living creature in the prospering development of our earth, and the cosmic system and our contribution to the system impacts its return to us. When we connect to this principle, we begin to love life not because we are such a small part of it, but because the connection to all living things surrounding us is so grand and magnificent that we can only wear its badge of gratitude for inviting us to join. Yes, this bountiful soil has traps and doors of disappointment and hurt, but the aliveness in all things is grander than its shadow, and the power to heal and thrive can be found in that vital connection.

While on a bush walk in Australia, I once found myself meditating on the lessons of our existential nature. During that time in my life, I was frequently asking for proof from the universe that there is a source of connection and communication between the elements and the human self. I wanted answers that tested the boundaries of academia, which had been such an integral part of my personal and professional life. I wanted to understand and feel beyond what science offered. I wanted to know more about why philosophers and writers, artists and spiritualists purported ideas that often seemed so opposed to our scientific way of understanding the world. As a clinician in the field of psychology, I knew these people were intuitively connected to planes of reality that professionals write off to subconscious access, or those outside of our field cast off with reductionist division about the arts versus the sciences. But deep down, the one thing I always knew was love, the only thing that does not discriminate between views but instead unites them. I allowed myself to move away from the righteousness of logic and embrace the judgements of letting them go. Thus, on that day in my meditative walk through the Australian bush, I tested the universe by asking it questions with the hope that I could connect to it, and it would answer me. And so, I asked the universe to teach me the truth about the cycle of life on earth. That seemed like a simple enough question. In my very next step on my walk, I came across a long bush of gardenias. Abundant and alive, the bush was mainly filled with green leaves. In the centre of the bush were four perfectly aligned gardenias. The first one was a beautiful bud in its infancy, the second was a gorgeous gardenia in full bloom, the third was a gardenia beginning to wilt and brown at the edges, and the last was one that had gone brown and listless. I marvelled with gratitude at the universe for this answer, this lesson, this reality that was a clear mirror with depth of truth beyond the surface of my question. On the one hand, I had found an answer that was delivered in my linear language: birth, youth, middle life and death. Most certainly, I was subconsciously asking about death, and more to the point, asking about life itself and where I was on the continuum. I could choose to see myself as one of those flowers. But beyond that was the entire life of the plant that supported it: the branches, the leaves, the soil, the roots, the sun, the ocean nearby. I realized in that moment that I wasn't just one of those flowers in a linear continuum of birth to death – I was the leaves, the air, the light, the earth, the soil, the water and the beautiful flower in all its iterations. In that moment, I saw the incredible aliveness, seen and unseen, that took place because the entire cycle of being was within this one plant. And through this connection were many lessons about all the existential questions we face. But the answers and lessons from the universe were larger than what I had asked. The lessons were about being – the embodiment of consciousness, the love of being. The answers and teachings were about our relationship not only to the elements, the earth and the universe; they were about the awakened journey that is beyond our sensory perception, articulation and mental programming. And yet, I was aware that this awakening manifested in an answer I could grasp within my human experience, and that a higher truth required a detachment from intellectual understanding. The wisdom of the plant did indeed come from its completeness, as I was able to communicate and simply be in its presence. We don't always need to communicate externally with the elements to find the answers we seek, especially when we realize that *we* are the elements themselves, and the elements are us. Hence, if we choose, we can communicate with the plants and other beings – and what secrets the bushes, the trees, the grasses, the knolls will tell you! Listen carefully, feel and connect to all that is alive in nature's essence. Know that what lives in that plant is as within the plant as it within you. That awakening will lead to a love of being.

Love of being is also an embodiment that is flooded with a multitude of dynamic feelings that lead us from our essence into the awareness of the aliveness of all things. Our job here on earth is to be in the full embrace of this love. What we see and feel beyond the body is also us, and that is truly sobering. Only then do we recognize that all things animate and inanimate are great reflections of who we experience ourselves to be. To embody love of being, we must continuously polish the reflections of our experiences by connecting to the truth of their lessons. Those lessons must then be used in profound ways that lead us to thrive in our aliveness. To not use our experiences is to allow them to mislead our destiny. That is what it means to be a lost soul. Love of being leads us to every experience with grace or stumbling, but also with full courage to trudge forward into life to live in our gifts.

Among our greatest gifts is the love of constantly being in this expression of humanity. We are here to feel it all. This is not something we can overlook or bypass. To truly love being, we must love the swinging tides of life that weave like an ineffable dream. Put it all together and maybe you can see a connection because that's how our linear minds organize thought. Watch your life from the perspective of being, and you will see it is a dream of scenes that rise and fall, ebb and flow with or without logic. No matter what, each moment is part of this inescapable state of essential being. This is indisputable love. When we only love the logic – the pieces that make sense – and translate it into a story of our minds' connection, we only love parts of our humanity. We have somehow decided that everything needs to make connected sense. But artists, dancers, dreamers and lovers know that inspiration is passionate, erratic, filled with highs and lows, and somehow all a part of their being. This embodiment requires our knowing that we are not here to be more than ourselves.

We are also here on earth to transcend our feelings into experienced dissolution of self and manifest destiny. So, how do we embody non-linear logic to fall into the love of being and manifest our destiny? How do we allow lessons that don't make rational sense to us, opinions that we don't find agreeable, and perspectives that distort our sense of who we are and why we thought we were here? Emotional transcendence is the road that leads us to letting go of our minds and falling into love of being. Thus, I suggest we love our thoughts and feelings as a part of our human journey. But we must also love them enough to let them go so that we can embody all our being. Transcendence is about stepping into the complete unknown and being on egoless terms with it. Only in this state can we embrace each other and our different ways of navigating being. When I don't know, I'm okay with you knowing your truth and your way – I can honour it because it is your way of being. And maybe your knowing and my unknowing together are true love. But when I know and you know and there is no room to unknow, there is division – not love.

Love of being includes our human experience. Our life experiences form the self, the answer to the question, "Who am I?" Those experiences weave a story of how I got from birth to now. The lessons from those experiences, however, dissolve the "Who am I?" into "I am." I am not this experience or that consequence. I am, as I was before this story began, a being of love itself. This ride of humanity is not about truths and untruths, gains and losses. It is about the journey of awakening to the presence of love as your being. To discover this gift, we must break down many of our colloquial notions about what it means to love and be loved. This deconstruction of love requires a departure from romanticized fairy tales of formulaic beginning, middle and end. The experience of love of being all that we are is in the fluidity, the back-and-forth, unsmooth journey of it all. Love of being includes a non-linear continuum of life experiences. There is no perfect order to life. There is today, right here, right now. In this moment, clean the river of your soul with awareness of every experience that has led you to this moment, so that you may lean into the river and see your reflection clearly. And when the river begins to move and carry your reflection, decide to follow it or to move away if your destiny does not follow the river. But know that you are also the river, the life within that river, and learn to love being the river.

CHAPTER 3

CONNECTED LOVE – THE THIRD DESTINY

I want to calm my soul beneath the rhythm of the sea,
Where only the waves remind me of my journey here,
A return to the womb before there was a me.
This was the crusade to life,
This thing we call human incarnation.
My soul knew it would be the fight for my spirit and all humanity,
To stay in this body and hear its dissonance of love and loss,
Every day the duality of the heavens beating the drum of the earth.
Ground me now in the song of your waters,
Where once I was one with your being,
And help me return to the beginning
With knowing I am here to live in all that is.
Hold my breath and bring me to stillness
And remind me to surface back to the atmosphere,
Where I am at once nourished by the elements,
Right here, right now,
In peace, on earth.
I return in full body within,
I live in full being within,
I love in fullness as one.

Connected love is our third destiny. It goes without saying that, much like our inextricability from nature, we cannot survive without connection to others. Thus, our relationships are not only here to provide procreation and companionship – our relationships are truly needed to expand our evolutionary process. Our relationships connect us to ourselves, nature, animals, family, partners and society, and they are reflections of our internal image of the world. This view shapes the way we experience trust, empathy, joy, freedom, compassion, contribution and a myriad of other realizations throughout our lives. Over the course of time, we have created a discourse for categorizing our relationship styles and even our own personality styles in order to better understand how we unite; hence, the popularity of comparing introversion versus extroversion, thrill seekers versus the risk averse, the ambitious versus the complacent, and so on. While all of these are most certainly captured on the continuum of psychological development, they are simply that: mere captures of how we relate based mostly on external influences. What we all share is our undeniable co-dependency on a world of deep connection that enables us to interweave loving relationships and personal freedom. I consider here that personal freedom is a very broad term not valued in all cultural settings, but I am more referring to the right to a life in which our way of connecting to our environment and others allows our minds, psyches and spirits to evolve with internal peace and joy while still holding a place for our pain and struggles. Our relationships have the capacity to truly raise our level of co-creation on this planet. When we recognize that relating is not a process of action but something that is already happening between us and all living things, we begin to understand the essence of our role here on earth. Our relation is intrinsic; therefore, the action is a reactive course that we can shape by raising our awareness of the interrelated connectivity between all living things. Respectively fashioned are our models of connection through the genders to which we identify. For example, masculine models of power, or feminine models that diminish masculinity, serve as division and miss the power of a true loving connection that allows us to relate and bond through love. A unification of the continuum of expression across the gender spectrum will allow for other expressions to arise and teach us more. At the same time, we can learn to cultivate our love of connection by working through some of our traditional relational models.

The love of connection through family relationships is something we've understood in terms of our psychological formation for some time. I won't repeat much of that psychology here but instead offer another perspective on this connection. I use the term "family" very loosely in this context, as I am mostly referring to our caregivers before life became of our own charge. Many of us are born into different constellations of family, and that too is part of our love destiny. But no matter who we got or didn't get during the time in our lives when we needed a caregiver's help, the platform was set for how we act out our lives. For most of us, this early period begins in a state of silence from within the waters of the womb. This silence is broken when we are born and become separate from this womb and, from that moment on, we begin needing connection for our survival. We spend the rest of our lives in the ebb and flow of this connection, it seems. Throughout our lives, we go through a series of metamorphic repetitions of birth and our need to connect by metaphorically returning home. We leave home and return home, day in and day out. We move from our parents' homes to our own homes, and the cycle repeats. We finish one phase of our lives only to be thrust into another. The connection toggles between ourselves and others. During this process, our families teach us to experience love in different ways. We are loved for the ways in which we behave, perform, accomplish, give, look, and so on. These lessons influence how we love and are loved, and we carry these lessons into our other relationships. I will emphasize here that critically deconstructing this process can be extremely useful in our development and is, in fact, a powerful process of coming into our own sense of love. However, for the purposes of this perspective on love and connection with our families, I would like to introduce the idea that because we are love, we are the experience of love before we even enter the constellation of our families; in other words, all that is necessary to be seen, heard and understood already exists. This stance enables a deeper familial connection, where love does not need to be shaped but is instead implicitly known and accepted. Rather than form love through our families, if we can be love and know that love is in our presence, our entire system of behavioural and social conditioning would shift. The scales of co-dependence between caregiver and child would change dramatically. The parent would operate under the assumption that cultivating connection means responding to that which already exists. The question of feeling loved would never even arise, and our families and societies would grow up with a deeper sense of knowing and being love.

Understandably, this is not the case in our current culture, and we continue to shape love through our family interactions. As such, it is important to work through the parts of those actions that shaped our definition and our sense of love. Of equal importance is our need to construct a connection to our intuitive definition and experience of being love. This full circle will help us return to our families with greater compassion and understanding and build the ultimate connection to them and ourselves. As such, we must continue to feed the waters of our internal river with nutrients, positivity and appreciation for it as it is and let it be love. We don't normally look at a river and wish it to flow in a different direction or motion. We don't look at the river and wish it to be another colour, another shape or another life. We look at the river and see a river and appreciate the river. But if you actively pollute the river, you can affect its life. And so, must we approach ourselves and our children with the awareness of the river as it is in all its naturism.

Love of connection through our partnerships will always be unfolding in our cultural narrative. This destiny is by far the evolutionary process of our heart into the road of the higher self. The highlight of partnership is not in finding agreement between two souls with shared point of view, but instead in seeing our partner's point of view and not reacting when it differs from our own. Only then can we see our partners wholly and appreciate so profoundly that it is them who offers us their fullness just as they are in every moment. These opportunities of relational differentiation help us to honour and accept one another without a desire to change them or their point of view. It is by disagreement without the need to pull our partners into our vision that we become closer and more wholly ourselves. How freeing it can be to run and play in partnership where difference is not simply tolerated, but instead appreciated and invited because we know that each difference is an opportunity to grow and love more honestly and profoundly.

The paradox here, of course, is that once we feel appreciation for our differences, the resistance caused by conflict dissipates, and agreement arises because you are no longer trying to change each other. You become mutually invested in loving yourselves and one another, as well as growing personally and relationally. This independent system of love is magic, because if you are both growing, you are not stagnant or complacent in your relationship, but instead actively participating in your evolution of connecting.

Allowing someone else to fully immerse themselves in the journey of who they are also allows us to expand our of notion of love. How do we do this? It's simple – we take the high road. This is not the road where you say and do the right thing so that you look good in your partner's eyes – and maybe even your own. The high road is the one that you climb with all your might, upon which you fall, scrape and curse through the pain, the suffering, the doubt, the fear, the anger, the sadness and the vulnerability and yet, you keep climbing. You do so because, at the top of this high road, you won't feel the pride of accomplishment, the bliss or the romance of it all, but instead you'll reach the zenith of a life lived in the nakedness of our truth. At the top, we find ourselves with all the story lines written on our skin, the invisible sutures of the heart, the ineffable hope that threads of gold run through our cells and unite our shadow with our light so that we may own and accept ourselves in love and finally let go. When we can share ourselves with another from this place of truth, we are connected, and only then can we experience intimacy.

There are flickers in the sky that make beautiful stars, and there is a spark so great it creates the light of the sun. Such light is more powerful than any momentary exchange and hotter than any moment of satisfaction. It's the law of attraction at its best that leads us to true intimacy. And true intimacy comes from seeing the wholeness of another in their light and in their shadow. We must scale the mountain of partnership with our strength and our vulnerability. We can't leave anything at the bottom hoping it will be forgotten. We must bring all of ourselves along the path to stay grounded and integrate into our connection.

Our love of connection to others is also vital to our understanding of the wholeness of human expression. This connection is paradoxical in that it seems to be our attraction to that which is outside of us, but is in fact the link to the ineffable, invisible connection between yourself and another. A great professor of mine taught me that most words in a conversation between two people are just noise – the vibration that is felt from heart to heart is the communication we are truly having. When we listen to another with our minds, the words get in the way – we either find them interesting or boring. When we listen with our hearts, we can fundamentally disagree or not have interest and still feel a connection. This is a connection of movement between souls that either heals us or destroys us. We must learn throughout our lives to listen from our hearts to expand our connections.

Throughout our lives, it's important to be selective about our social relationships. However, for better or for worse, it seems we subconsciously choose those from whom we need to learn. Sometimes we awaken to the lessons of these connections, and sometimes we just seem to find the same people over and over. This psychological interpretation is a valuable one, but I share it cautiously in that it puts the onus on us to change our relationship with ourselves in order to attract different people. Arguably, this is certainly one aspect. But coming from the early perspective of ourselves as pure love wired for connection, what you radiate becomes not only an aura toward others that automatically draws in those people, but it also creates a layer of non-emotional reactivity toward those who cannot reflect in ways we find acceptable. In other words, we don't get hooked. It's easy to dislike or hate. But to feel the unpleasantness and use the feeling critically to see the heart behind the presentation is an opportunity to connect. This is not to say that you must actively engage with every human being you come across and dislike, but it does create a passage for your life as you will traverse so many relationships in so many contexts. It's not only about being authentic, or being your best self around others, it's about getting out of yourself so that the waters of your rivers become clear once again, allowing you to see the souls beneath are all on the course to their own destiny, too.

Our growth potential is infinite, and so is the wisdom in our souls. The more you allow relationships to grow, the clearer and more fulfilled the soul becomes. Love of connection is truly divine.

Connecting through the self is the foundation of connection to all. We are in relationships with everyone and to everything. And there are many methods for cultivating our connection. The first step is learning to listen from within ourselves. This is a skill in and of itself. Sometimes, we can develop this skill by first listening externally. Nature is always speaking to us. First, we must open ourselves to the relationship with nature and, before speaking, actually listen. Listen to the winds, the trees, the animals, the hum of the earth. From there, we can draw nature's sounds inward and notice. There is a heart that beats with a rhythm and flow that is magical. This is a form of meditation that allows connection. Furthermore, while meditation is one truly powerful way to connect, the definition of what is meditative is quite broad. Some people can listen by sitting in nature, while others can listen from the comfort of a nice sofa. Some may listen by running, others by praying, and then there are some who hear while carving wood, tinkering, painting, singing or watching the sun go down.

Finally, and most importantly, we must learn to love freely. We cannot determine how our family members choose to live their lives any more than we can force our partners to change. Each person has their own path for travelling to their love destiny. Whatever presents in each person's path is theirs to heal and ours to love. This means that we offer what we have within our resources, but we allow what they have within theirs to guide them through their challenges, their triumphs and their life. To truly love anyone in their wholeness, we must love them in a way that shows that we trust their journey is as much their own as it is ours. This release can be difficult because our nature is to attach and control outcomes. But an evolved heart knows it cannot control love – it can only allow it.

CHAPTER 4

ANCESTRAL LOVE –
THE FOURTH DESTINY

The ancestors whispered of transcendence of their spirits.
They made imprints on the path of life's dust that
brought us to this moment.
Those imprints were the lessons of inspiration and
progress, error and agony.
The ancestors whispered forgiveness from their hearts,
illuminating forgiveness in our own.
Those actions made imprints of dust that create this moment.
Those lessons released our hearts and elucidated our callings.
The ancestors whispered gratitude for the torch of life we carry.
Those imprints cleared time and wiped away all our fears.
Those lessons brought courage and compassion to our being.
The ancestors whispered of love.
Those imprints healed what only we could erase.
Those lessons ignited passion of the heart,
awakening the flame of all love,
And we bowed to the ancestors with all our tears of
sadness and joy.
Those lessons lifted the burdens of life.
Those imprints cleared the legacy we left behind.
Our legacy became love.

The fourth destiny is ancestral love. The lineage of those that came before us is an inextricable and unknown part of ourselves. This road of collective inheritance has created the world as we know it. The shadow and light of our transformation have come from the paths paved by our ancestors. Their construction is a direct energetic lineage that provides us with information about our psychological stagnation and progression. That personal devolvement extends to all future generations and thus into society. An exploration of ancestral inheritance can lead to a deeper understanding of our incarnation and arguably our biopsychosocial (biological, psychological and social) makeup.

As hunters and gatherers, we had a natural connection to the earth and the elements, but as we became gardeners and planters, we changed the landscape of that connection. Over time that relationship grew into one of mass production, and we grew as a population. In order to sustain the growing populations, we industrialized ourselves in a way that suppressed our ancestry. And while much was gained in the process, much was also lost. By integrating our scientific disciplines, we are continuously discovering and learning about technologies and civilizations we have lost. We must continue to examine the consequences of what we discard in the name of progress. Among such consequences is our deep connection to the land – the habitat that is our great gift of life – and to those fewer tangible connections of spirit and heart. Sometimes such connections to wisdoms and traditions become marginalized into categories of non-academic value. They have often been devalued by judgement of that which cannot be proven. Thus, this is a story about the destinies of love which happen through your personal evolution; therefore, this is not an academic exercise in rationalization, but instead a destiny of integrating past, present and future through the space of your heart.

Now, modernization is not evil. It is, in fact, beautiful, hopeful and necessary. Much of this progression is intended to support our planetary growth. But like all things, this adaptation has boundaries. We are thus in a time of learning about those boundaries between nature and humanity. An examination of our ancestral legacies can help us to re-construct useful connections that became subjugated through our modernization so that we may revive the interconnectivity between earth's power, its gifts and ourselves in order to advance and expand from a place of greater honesty, integration and clear connection. We have not lost our way; the ancestral links are within and accessible to us. Cultivating ancestral connections opens us into the sensory realm of their offerings so that we may uplift ourselves and our world.

Another aspect of ancestral love examines the way in which humans have severed themselves from one another. Through many generations, individuals have separated emotionally and physically from family members, friends or their homelands. We have severed society through wars and other human-made catastrophes. Some cut-offs have been less intentional, such as disease, starvation or natural disaster. Whatever that throughline, the story that leads to our personal narrative gives us a deeper understanding not only of how we came to be, but how we are now, shut off from certain aspects of ourselves. For this to occur, a process of reunion between ourselves and our ancestors can be helpful so that we may heal their inherited wounds and transform the healing within ourselves. This process of awareness creates a bridge of love to the legacies of our ancestors; by crossing it, our appreciative exploration leads to a fluid connection with our past, one that allows expansion. It is through this process that we begin to recognize that we are a part of the whole, and the whole is not only greater than the sum of its parts, but it is whole on its own.

With the understanding that we can only go so far back in our literal learning of ancestral history, there is also learning about history itself on a larger scale that can help us intuitively tap into the subconscious feelings we hold. Some come to us through ancestral lineage, and some are part of the collective memory we inherit. Ancestral love becomes a retrieval of lost parts of ourselves and the world as we know it. It is a reclamation different from the historical perspective provided by media or books – it is one of intuition, of sensory memory we are not accustomed to tuning into. While this may sound esoteric in nature, what is more factual is opening up to the possibility that we do inherit memory and knowing, similarly to how we might inherit biological health markers. This paradigm shift can aid us in recognizing and acknowledging our intuitive senses. There are many books and varied cultural rituals for ancestral work. But the idea here is to find your own way into a connection of genuine curiosity, critical feeling and vital connection of your lineage to the ancestral world that was here before you, the one that welcomed your soul into creation. Consider yourself an explorer of journeys, treasures, secrets, myths and even truths. Allow your body to speak to you and listen. Rather than writing off a sense – such as having been somewhere you've never visited or belonging to something you've never experienced – listen attentively. Sit with the message and allow the feeling to communicate the possibility of inherent knowledge, a lesson, an instinct that perhaps cannot be proven but is worthy of acknowledgement. Validating and attending to your own feelings is the ultimate way to nurture your senses. It is the healing path to learn the human gift of feeling. It is one of the highest schools of our incarnation. This personal way of listening, learning, acknowledging and validating our sense of truth gives rise to our interconnectedness, and our existential alchemy becomes a path that leads to our destiny.

Still, ancestral love is more than the silver chord of your past. It also the imprint of your present. When we connect to ancestral love, we clear the weeds of our past and learn from what we have inherited. We learn to honour our past by integrating what we have inherited into our being, rather than discarding or suppressing it as bad, antiquated or useless. Those who came before us to walk this earth were souls on their path. What and how they lived – joy and trauma alike – is an experience from which we can draw lessons to liberate ourselves from those chains and, in turn, free those around us by becoming our highest selves. This integration is a process of love that shapes our contribution here on earth and the way we manifest those contributions. That is to say, when we look at our past wholly from a learner's point of view, we can better empathize with our feelings and the feelings of others. Whether our ancestors were heroes or villains, ordinary or extraordinary, their time became our time, and we are here now to live in a connected state where we can assume our path, grow and let go. Taking this road liberates our souls into our natural way. Furthermore, this creates a legacy for those who come after us that is free of toxic constructions and leaves that same path clear for their souls to evolve. Our legacy then turns to one of ancestral love, through which we recognize we are because we have always been a part of an incomparable essence of love and, as such, will continue to be.

Joining our inherited history through sensory intuition melds the psyche and the soul because, at a heart level, we develop our healing beyond intellectual understanding. Instead, we do so in a way that invokes gratitude and forgiveness, which leads to clarity and surrender. Whether we know it or not, on a subconscious level, we carry the wounds of our ancestors through our religions, books, stories and dialogues. The only way to impact the direction of that discourse is by discovering that what was in our ancestors is also in us. Perhaps it has evolved, transformed or transmuted, but nonetheless it is a silver chord of remembrance uniting all beings. In order to understand this concept, we must make a departure from the idea that we are either good or bad, selfish or selfless, careful or careless. We must look further into the heart of the actions that enabled systems of fear or, alternatively, activated systems of love. Systems of fear are meant to regulate, while systems of love are meant to liberate. Fear is bound in time and space, but love is not. So, the ability to understand those inherited parts of our ancestry and integrate them into our being allows us to connect to who we are in this very moment of breath and aliveness. That integration is love, and that love is your freedom.

One of my favourite quotes comes from *The Alchemist* by Paulo Coehlo. The main character, a shepherd boy, is asked in his travels if he learned anything from the books lent to him by an Englishman. The boy replies, "I learned that the world has a soul, and that whoever understands that soul can also understand the language of things."

The soul of our ancestors has left a vibratory imprint that is interwoven with our own. That imprint is the soul of the world. And, as the boy goes on to discover, "...the soul is made of love." When we think of the world as having a soul, the consciousness of our individual soul is expanded. We begin to realize that exploring and cultivating a loving relationship with our soul is a part of the coherence of the life we experience. This coherence has the potential to create a connection to the ineffable awareness that permeates all existence. It is infinite, boundless love.

In the ancient Hawaiian healing system of Ho'oponopono, this state of love is sometimes referred to as the zero state. The zero state is likened to a blank slate, on which shadows and imperfections do not exist. It is clear light, the God state, where good and bad and thoughts and feeling perceptions do not exist. It is simply the divine state of consciousness – the language of things. That life force or consciousness is, was and will always be, and we have an impact on how connected we are to its vibration by how we remain in alignment to our source of connection.

CHAPTER 5

SPIRITUAL LOVE – THE FIFTH DESTINY

As I soared and I travelled, I felt a warm embodiment
of another cosmos;
As if I lived or belonged to a realm where the
planets were golden,
A system of light.
It wasn't our planetary system –
It was higher, further, more vibrant.
I flew so high and so free
And connected at a higher level than ever before.
It made me sad to shed what I had held onto for so long
that kept me so bound.
I felt like a body of light that felt more at home than
I have ever been,
And then a book of soul wisdom was handed to me.
This was my love destiny
And so, I returned.

The fifth destiny is spiritual love. Spiritual love is our connection to the ineffable timelessness that is our inner divinity. This is a knowledge that goes beyond observable reality. In the space of spiritual love, there is a departure from the polarity of just and unjust, true and untrue, virtuous and wicked, known and unknown. Spiritual love is a learning about the dissolution of egoic notions of concrete thought identification. This means that everything you think yourself to be according to what you have learned or have been told you were dissolves through your learning path. I feel, I touch, I see, I smell, I hear are divine pathways through the ego into the expanse of the infinite. In essence, the expedition of ethereality or spiritual love is one of intricate reclamation of the spirit within us all.

In psychology we spend much of our time developing the ego. I refer to the ego here as the healthy centre of self-identity that is balanced in its own thoughts, emotions and behaviours. From a Western perspective, this development of self continues to be useful. Developing and knowing the ego self helps us form an identity within our culture so that we can function with a sense of belonging, worth and connection. The formation of this self-image remains a healthy way to come to know who we are as individuals within the constructs of our families and society. Meanwhile, most of this formation is developed by our rearing, education and societal influences. An exploration or further development of the self is offered by the field of psychology. Traditional psychotherapies are the prevailing medicine to help us navigate a healthy ego formation outside of the one shaped by our upbringing. This process can be valuable in discovering and reshaping who we think we are. But therapy is only one of those ways and is most certainly a preference that is not a one-size-fits-all path. How we find who we are in the earth sense of ego is a multi-faceted road of options in our human experience. It is equally important to recognize that many cultures value a more collective development of the sense of "I" and that some cultures do not define self through individualism. Therefore, ego development in the Western sense does not have to take place. The work beyond the western "I" is an amalgamation of self-love, and the journey of love beyond the self becomes the work of our lives for a deeper connection that takes us out of our minds and helps us journey into the quantum field of psychological freedom.

Spiritual love is simply a way of discovering the heart of our true being beyond the limits of the mind. For many, the term "spirituality" is connected to religion or some pagan image of worship and laden with imprints of how things are or should be. Spiritual love begs a new definition of the term spirituality. This initially requires a road of self-education where, regardless of what you were taught, you begin to explore and expand your own learning about the quandary and query of life's questions, meaning and purpose. This learning leads to a cultivation and construction of practices of your own choice, will and desire that help you to discover your own spiritual love destiny. However, if your spiritual destiny is an inherited one that fulfils the cultivation of your soul's purpose, that too is to be honoured through awareness and gratitude.

Pope Frances said, "*El amor es gratuito, o no es amor,*" which translates to "Love is free, or it is not love." In the process of discovery, spiritual love allows for doubt, scepticism, struggle and rejection of ideas that seem foreign, new or unexplainable. It is a true unconditional love that allows all thoughts, feeling and judgements to pass through us. The unconditional nature of true love allows all aspects of thought and feeling in order to transmute them. It is true that some describe this love as their intrinsic sense of God, Source, Oneness, the Great Life Force. But it is my position that this is a most intimate definition that we are invited to label or not label at all.

Like all loves, spiritual love can be one that has a slow process of unfolding for some, whereas for others it is a one-pointed path. What is essential to the development of this destiny is a space within our culture for this exploration and cultivation of love to occur. It is not until we give ourselves the permission to experience life beyond what is offered in the physical world that we can begin this great adventure. And then, how your spirituality is designed, practised or lived can have great variance. That is the beauty of spiritual love. It is not tolerance or acceptance – it is unification of existing personal and universal truths and truths beyond. This journey requires patience; it requires an unfolding of love itself.

Life often teaches us to build layers of protection about how the world is and what role we are to play in it. For many this evolves into a road of survival where we lose ourselves and the great connection within. So how do we build a culture that allows us to create spiritual love? Look around and simply observe without judgement the many books, philosophies, religions, ideologies, practices, arts and sciences, and find in them what humanity seeks. It is up to you and only you to determine the road you take internally. You are the only one, the one that lives in your heart, and therefore the only one that can live out your heart's destiny. Thus, this path does not exclude one's religion or ways – this destiny includes finding where your soul meets your heart into love.

Spiritual love is a path of attempting to understand how the universe works in order to clearly see what we were born knowing, and uniting with the energy of this state. When this understanding occurs, we can feel an alignment happening that shifts our way of understanding love. But this requires a further departure, a departure of linear thinking. Our experience of love is non-linear, yet we seem to only be able to explain in linear language. This paradox is revealing because it leads us to wonder how non-linear experience can be captured into our way of being in the world. We love evidence, but not all things are evidenced, and yet they are somehow experienced. Medical doctors know this well. They are taught frameworks from which they formulate diagnoses, but they are not taught frameworks to capture the role of shared experience with their patients' well-being. In psychology, the healing that clients experience from the connection to their therapists can never truly be captured, and so we refer to it as the art of therapy, as opposed to the science. Hence, while our minds may discover other ways to capture information and explain it with logic, we must take a leap of faith that there is knowing from within our hearts' profundity, and it possesses a capacity to love that is beyond linear logic.

From this place, our understanding begins to merge into an awareness. This awareness brings to the surface what we think we know and what we notice. It also allows us to swim in the waters of what we don't know and learn to build a relationship with the unknown. This awareness can be nurtured. The awareness of spiritual love can be developed through meditation, prayer or contemplation. For some, it will occur through song, dance, art or the written word.

Rituals that are tradition or self-created can help us in grounding this love into a celebration of self-attendance. How loved we feel when we are truly attended to! Our hearts begin to soften and the pulse of vitality within us becomes well-being. Spiritual love is true well-being.

Dr Wayne Dyer, the internationally renowned author and speaker in the fields of self-development and spiritual growth, taught that we don't manifest through wishful thinking reflected by simple desire or wanting, but that instead, "We manifest what we are." Part of manifesting this aspect of our destiny requires raising our vibration. He recommended reading the great works and scriptures from multiple traditions, sages, philosophers, poets. These documents often hold lessons that inspire us, or as he might put it, help us "…to be in spirit." This space in spirit is the ultimate surrender. To relinquish the mind, we must surrender to our hearts. Here, we become inspired to be our very best selves, living in an awakened state of consciousness. In this state we merge into the completeness with the great unknown.

For many, reading about spirituality alone is like trying to read a meditation. It's a bit difficult to translate from the written word something that is meant to be experienced beyond words. But reading can help spark a new thought or feeling that we can then use to sit with. The beauty of this perspective is that it allows us to approach our thoughts and feelings from a totally different angle than the one of reacting from instinct. Next time you come across a word or a phrase or a piece of advice, jot it down on a piece of paper and place it in front of you. Allow yourself to read it, ponder it, feel it so it all flows through you. And then, allow the words to simply sit on the piece of paper, in front of you, outside of you. Imagine for a moment that those words can hold all their meaning and symbolism on that paper without you. Now, close your eyes for a moment and go internally empty of the words. If they come back, simply remember they are at home on that paper at this moment. Return, go inward, sit and notice what surfaces. Some things that surface are strange, others uncomfortable, some bothersome, others noisy. Just sit and allow whatever is there to be there. The more you practise this, the more you will learn to empty the mind and the body of those words dominating your instinctive reactions. If you are patient enough, the meaning and power of those words will eventually transform within you – as will your experience. When this transformation occurs, you become more connected because the words are not controlling you, and you are not controlling them. A simple symbiotic experience is happening between you and them. This allows you to come from a more honest place within yourself and see and feel and surrender to whatever is. This emptiness can bring you answers and deep solace.

The whole process is spiritual because it is you attending to the you that is within. This requires kindness and patience toward yourself. If you feel frustrated or worried or angry, can you put those feelings on another piece of paper and, after allowing yourself to feel them, let them sit outside of you and be? If you feel bliss, elation or love, can you put them on another piece of paper and let them sit outside of you and be? This is the freedom of not having to attach an outcome or an experience to words, feelings and thoughts: you are in the alignment of the loving space within you, where words and thoughts are not who you are, but perhaps simply what you experience. The minute you attach to any of those experiences as being real – and by real, I mean controlling your emotion in some way – you've disconnected. So, come back with the words you would speak to a young child in need and say the things that child needs to hear. Say them, literally. Put those words on a piece of paper, hold that paper to your heart and then place it before you and sit once more within yourself. This is the path of spiritual love.

As previously mentioned, the destiny of spiritual love is for some a straight path to the divinity within them. They are born living this destiny, and these people can be a source of wisdom, inspiration and guidance. For others it is a more circuitous route. But there are teachers in our lives, and they are like the stars that guide ships, illuminating our way. It is wonderful to allow yourself to learn by listening to others. In some indigenous cultures, many of the wisdom teachings came through sharing accounts of the community's day. This was often done through storytelling, which could give even the most mundane experience a new perspective, power or lesson. Finding your community – that is to say, people who help you tell your story in a way that honours it, become the audience who sees it, applaud it, laugh with it, cry with it, mourn it, nurture it, value it and love it – helps. We are relational beings. We depend on connections from the moment we are born. Those connections wire our brains and sustain us in living. And so, it is helpful to find those people, the council that helps us make those connections by supporting your growth, your quest, your story. To this end, it is also profoundly important to be aware that you can get stuck and not flow through love in this destiny if you put all your power in those teachers. You admire, learn, glean and love them so that they may become the clearest mirrors that reflect your soul. These mirrors do not want for themselves; instead, they may enjoy the path of sharing, teaching and guiding, but they ultimately allow you to be the master of your own destiny. Otherwise, what they offer is not love. When someone does their internal work, they become a clear mirror that holds space for darkness and still reflects back your light, your essence, you. A teacher does not want or seek your approval, adulation or following; they simply love you enough for you to become your own teacher and master of your love destiny.

This destiny is one of a sacred time in your life. You may find in this phase that you feel your energy turned inward. This is often a time of reflection, discovery and a shift into the query of accepting a deeper aspect of who you are. To navigate this destiny is destiny itself unfolding, melting through the layers of the heart that have been shaped, hardened and even wounded by the human experience and the ego's influence. During this evolution, your attention to clearing out emotional cobwebs becomes essential to your path. This can be aided by nature.

Nature can help ground you as she holds you in her womb to rebirth a version of you that is the breath itself. This is a time to take off your shoes and feel the earth beneath your feet. Allow your hands to feel the leaves, grasses, bark, petals. Breathe in the scents of herbs, flowers, earth. Listen to the sounds beyond the sounds of urban life so that you may reset your senses to the natural state they were in at your birth. Being deliberate in this stage is the first step. You must cultivate a routine that endorses and supports these pockets of connection as a priority in your life. I've read many soft and kind suggestions for bringing healing practices into your life, but at the end of the day, they are practices. They require your time, your attention, your dedication, your devotion, your faith and, ultimately, your love. To many, this is where the destiny is curtailed. The time and devotion seem too imposing for a modern world; however, the opposite is possible by allowing this destiny to unfold. It is possible that these practices bring you into an unexpected journey of awakening. This awakening may help reveal the purpose beyond your purpose. It can turn your whole world so that where you thought you were going is different from where you know you are meant to be. It is the sleeping giant in your heart. Once awakened, it cannot be undone or taken from you. Our habits can turn them off, but what is known cannot be unknown. And when we know that we can begin to love ourselves in this way, our window of consciousness broadens. Here, we can raise our vibration into the inevitable and ubiquitous expansion of our incarnation: love. Spiritual love is a new realm of love. What your realm reveals is your school and your gift. It is your spiritual love journey.

One of the key helpers in this destiny is to learn to become boundless by becoming comfortable with the unknown, the unprovable, the undoable, the unachievable. What you believe you do not have or cannot have or do, becomes an entanglement of limitations. And once you think you don't fit in or there isn't room for you, there isn't. Therefore, this destiny requires that you develop a departure from right and wrong... and knowing. This will allow you to travel into incorporeality – that is, the non-physical, non-material or three-dimensional way of seeing things. The issue here is that it is yet another layer of releasing and surrendering ideas, lessons and notions you may have acquired. So, you do all this studying, seeking, searching and soul finding, and now you must let it all go? One might ask, what is the point? But it's amazing how we blossom when we are truly free. Indeed, our hearts become boundless. Releasing one's ideas of knowledge dissolves barriers between all human beings. Through this emptiness you may find that you are able to connect with all beings – somewhere, somehow, beyond differences, beyond every fibre of hierarchy, the only conquering left will be the conquering of your heart! In there lies a boundless universe where reality isn't known or defined by time; it is simply boundless, infinite, vast love.

Spiritual love requires a deep process of forgiveness. When we forgive, we take full responsibility for ourselves on a whole new level. We take full responsibility for how our thoughts, actions and feelings affect our lives and, therefore, the lives of others. To forgive ourselves of our errors, our judgements and our injuries is not to excuse or allow a repetition; it is to clear the path of the heart with love. It means to love anyway. In essence, it means saying to yourself, "I refuse to abandon my path to love because of this pain. I forgive myself for how I've contributed in thought, action, inaction or judgement. I forgive myself for how I stood in my own way or the way of others. I forgive myself because I take full responsibility and know now that forgiveness is a path of responsibility." Only then can we make amends. And in order to amend, we must forge a path of love, which is in each of us. Essentially, forgiveness is a road of loving action toward the self.

To this end, spiritual love is the destiny of healing. The great Master Mikao Usui, who is known as the father of the healing system of Reiki, discovered a system to connect and utilize the power of consciousness, or what is referred to as the universal life force. Through his studies and meditational journey, Usui Sensei discovered that one could connect to the universal life force in order to move oneself into a healed or whole state. The premise is that humans fall out of alignment with the life force energy and fall into physical, mental or emotional unease. By coming into alignment with the universal life force, we can heal ourselves and live in an aligned state. Usui Sensei did not claim to create the life force, as it was already there, but he developed a method for energetically connecting to it and a language for allowing that connection to move through us and return us to our natural state of wholeness. Simplified, spiritual alignment leads to a harmonious state. A harmonious state is that place where we love ourselves freely, and that love emanates in a flowing cascade of brilliant harmony.

CHAPTER 6

AWAKENING LOVE – THE SIXTH DESTINY

She felt something divine coming her way,
A sudden orientation,
Glimpses of serenity and bliss,
That day when the vibrancy of the sun and trees and the
light of the day reminded her
That she had been hibernating in an illusion of love,
Followed by the daydream of infinite white sands and glorious stars
That spoke in a cry by the night's expanse
And swallowed her whole.
This was not a sudden awakening;
It was a slow unfolding
Of countless veils lifting and revealing visions of dusk and dawn,
With momentary mirages of yellow brick roads
And thunderous butterflies fluttering in the rainforests.
Her heart cracked open with the pain of birth
And what a gift it was.
Freedom and elevation that all is and will always be well within her.

Throughout our lives, we feel we know what love is by how it is
demonstrated to us and how we experience it. This definition
becomes a collection of stories, images and practices that result in
a surrender to what we think we have learned about it. This is a
limiting experience, as it creates fantasies that we try to imitate or

recreate in order to fit into the definition we have of love. However, love is a boundless state that exists in the intrinsic nature of the heart when it is open to our inner light. When we know this, we are in an awakened state of love.

Sometimes, our life journey begins in trauma, but that does not remove the light that was you before you entered the human journey. That journey often seems confusing as it enters and exits the caves of emotion. Plain and simple, life is not meant to be without feeling; it is meant to be a school of learning from our emotions. Those emotions are metaphors that guide us into the highest emotion a human can feel. But that emotion is not one thing. From the tree of love extend the many branches of compassion, kindness, empathy, care, passion, excitement, sorrow and pain, just to name a few of an endless gamut of feelings. Love is all those things. Each branch is a limb of life that propels us to grow toward the light. That light is not above, but deeply within where its brilliance holds warmth over our souls and connects us forever to our hearts. In this awakening we become clear, aligned, purposeful – the full embodiment of who we are.

Nevertheless, the process of knowing who we are is often one of retrieval of what has become hidden within us – our boundless state of being love. Imagine being taught that you are love and always will be. Imagine being taught to speak to your heart and learn its language before being asked what you want to do or be? This language exists and is the most powerful among us. It is a language beyond words that, when nurtured, can become the brilliant awakening of our incarnation. This language exists in silence, where the glint of another's eyes or the touch of another's hand dawns our existential birth, because here we are completely connected. We are one – this is love.

Some are born awake, but for most, our process of enculturation lulls them into a subconscious existence. Hence, this destiny is one of patience, seeking, commitment and allowing the mind to shift from being the commander of your life to being the dedicated companion of your heart, so the illusion that they are separate from each other begins to fade. In the awakening of the heart, a new layer of life unfolds because it makes us deal with our past by acknowledging it, valuing it and understanding it. Awakening also makes us deal with the future – the world of worry, uncertainty and death. When we explore this future and make peace with our powerlessness over it, we enter the path of commitment to love.

In the here and now, we become connected to our hearts – that is the destiny of love. To live this destiny in its entirety, we must be willing to nourish our hearts so deeply that our vision broadens to the point where we can see life in everything. The road starts wherever you seek, so long as it is in the intention of joining your heart from the depths of your highest self.

To join this path, we must first practise returning to the nonverbal state in which we entered this world. I remember the hours of silence with my newborn daughter in the first few months of her life. As I dressed her, fed her and cuddled her, I saw her big, brown eyes looking back at me as she sat in hours of her silence by my side. I remember a moment when I came into the awareness that this time would pass, and this meditation-in-action in which she lived would no longer be. The awareness became a meditation, a conscious awakening and a paradigm shift for me. It was powerful. I remembered that we were all once that silent child. So, there are moments in my days when I practise returning to that place within me that lived in the presence of silence. We must practise putting the brakes on our words from time to time. Sit with you in your heart and nourish the arising thoughts by acknowledging them and loving them enough to let them go. Practise playing with nature and asking it to send you messages and then letting the expectations go. Practise reading a few words or whole texts that inspire you and then let them be. Practise doing nothing and remind yourself that right here, right now, doing nothing is your connection to your inner being where you intuitively remember and become love once more.

In this destiny, we also become aware of old habits, thought patterns, even unconscious beliefs and understandings we have within ourselves. These unconscious influences literally interfere with our life dreams. While we may get up in the morning thinking we know exactly what we are going to do to get ourselves closer to our dreams or even put us in alignment with them, we constantly find ourselves redirected to other matters. We make lists, talk, read and learn about what we must do to realize our life goals, but along the way, we get busy, stuck or rerouted in a pattern that keeps us from reaching those dreams and the dreams beyond the ones we thought we wanted. This goes on and on, keeping us from realizing the magnificence of our creation, our potential and our ability to manifest our dreams. Therefore, we must use our longing and seeking to become aware of the ways that help us, and undo the ways that hinder us from living in the presence of love. We must explore and confront our fears, our anger, disappointments and even rage, so we can return to the immersion of an awakening so profound it makes us whole.

This is an intimate process. It is a process of self-discovery that requires not only consciously facing your demons, but also facing your light. We have selective minds that, throughout our lives, weave truths that are a lot like our sleep dreams. Our memories are full of holes, omissions and even distortions – good and bad. Delving into these story lines helps us better understand the impact of those memories and how asleep or awake we really are, which allows us to live in a way that is unobstructed by our past. We tend to lean toward the more painful and negative memories and hail positive highlights as outstanding moments. This limits our ability to imagine a world of memories woven with only outstanding moments. This isn't to suggest a rose-coloured viewpoint that is devoid of life's difficulties; it is instead a cultivation of memories that include outstanding moments to support us even in tough times. This process helps us to understand and put things into a place of balance so that we can move through them and broaden our awareness.

When I used to teach psychology to graduate students, I often gave them a speech at the beginning of a class before introducing a new theory. I would say, "The theory you are about to learn is new information and a departure from the traditional psychology you have learned. For some of you, it may be a shift in what you thought psychology to be. But my hope is to inspire your learning not by teaching you this theory as a truth, but as a window that opens a bit and sheds a new ray of light on what you have already learned so that you may create and define your own psychological truth." Because often when we learn something new about life, ourselves and our ways, we feel as if we must ignore what we did before. This is not the case. We must integrate what came before and use it so we can let it go.

This process is indeed a mission of love because it requires grieving truths with which we have often identified for our whole lives. And when we begin to shed these old truths, we can become overwhelmed by sadness, loss and disorientation. This is a normal part of the process. It's a lot like leaving childhood behind, only to realize your responsibility as an adult is larger than you could have imagined. Therefore, we must grieve by honouring our past through our process of awakening.

Faith in love is the real awakening. For that is the spirit awakening to the higher consciousness within us. Once we've looked at our past to understand the road we are paving – only to find ourselves in the here and now – we awaken to the only thing left to carry us in this evolution. Faith is trust that you've dealt and are dealing with your all the noise, the notions, the nothings that we thought were somethings. Our awakening calls for a leap of faith but, because we have done our work to reconcile this identity, we can surrender to the idea that somewhere beyond our control is a harmonious state of breath that is a direct channel to the divine. What you deem as divine is truly personal and, therefore, to be defined by you, but it is found within us all. Deep in the brilliance of our heart is the unfathomable hollowness beyond time and space where there is no need for sleep.

As a therapist, I find that my work with clients has been reflected by my own awakening, creating a channel that illuminates their path to the same enlightenment. Each client is profoundly unique. Their life stories are magnificent, even when they don't see it that way. Their personal perspectives and feelings all tell of a life journey in search of understanding, validation and insight into their existence. It takes great courage to be a client. It means trusting a total stranger whose intention for coming into this line of work is not often known to the client. And yet, clients make the leap of faith for their own well-being to find that place within where life aligns harmoniously.

I love so many of the psychological theories that take therapists into the frameworks that attempt to help us understand the human experience, but I know in my heart of hearts that the healing does not happen through what I know – it happens through the connection we create together. When a client and therapist are a match and the work takes off, it means that our hearts are communicating at a subconscious level. This level occurs in the shedding of layers that lie beneath the words, the tasks, the analysis. This occurs through the confluence of two souls that have come together perfectly to link their hearts into healing. The therapist believes she or he has come to help someone who needs their guidance. The client believes they need help and hopes the therapist can provide that for them. So, here you have two souls who have engaged in a reality, a construct that says, "If we join, I can be whole". But that wholeness is only lost or perhaps blurred by a known or unknown memory that is creating a blockage, or a lesson that one needs in order to grow. The wholeness of the client already exists. The therapist entering the agreement, on some level, is not whole themselves because they believe they are a conduit to finding the equilibrium that makes the client whole. When the therapist surrenders this reality, clients will no longer exist. But both therapist and client are inextricably entangled in the human experience of thoughts and feelings.

Therapists are often taught that, in order to truly help another person, they must become a blank slate. That is, the therapist must become so clear that the only thing the client can see in them is themselves. To this day, this aspect of therapeutic work continues to be of great value. But how does a therapist become so enlightened that they are truly a blank slate? We don't. Therapists are humans full of humanity and all it entails. So, each therapist continues to clean their slate repeatedly by doing their own work to become clearer for the client. I clean my slate by awakening to love – not the kind of love we know as mother love, child love, friend love or partner love, but awakened love. It's the state of awareness of all that another human is experiencing and expressing, and that healing means returning to the source of love that was my nature before life told me who I was. There, my slate is clear and bright and open. And in those apertures of my heart, I can reflect, even in brief moments, so perhaps the client can clearly see the best of themselves. I am also open to the converse or the meeting of both. Perhaps it is they who are letting me into their hearts, or we are both connecting in that channel of light, heart to heart – either way, we awaken love. As the great Guru Ram Dass put it, "Souls love. That's what souls do."

My story of awakening was not sudden. It was a series of unveilings throughout my life and continues to be. One such unveiling came many years ago during a conversation with a childhood friend, Steven. He lived with muscular dystrophy from the age of six and was bound to a wheelchair for most of his life. He had a brilliant mind, sharp wit, contagious laughter and a way of saying exactly what he meant. We rarely had conversations that felt superficial, as they just felt like truth laced with sarcasm, laughter and humour to help it all go down. And it wasn't just one conversation alone that was an awakening – it was the way in which Steven spoke about his own life with complete candour, never holding back. The limitation he experienced in his body was extraordinarily surpassed by his unparalleled commitment to achieve what many never will: kindness when he spoke and his absolute acceptance of his reality. At six feet tall, with an infectious smile and echoing laughter, he was a big presence, and anyone who knew him knew it.

I remember one day we spoke in earnest about our views on life, afterlife and what living the day meant for each of us at the time. I was telling him my story of why I had decided to go back to school for my psychology degree. I mentioned how limited I had felt by my first career and that I knew all along I had to face returning to the books. I said this to the guy who became an astrophysicist without being able to move more than a finger on his hand. He chuckled almost mockingly and said, "Of course you're a therapist, that's what you always wanted to be." I was baffled by his comment and the certainty of his tone, especially because I knew he was rarely wrong. I asked him what he meant, and he recalled a conversation we had when were younger when I told him I wanted to be a speech therapist and help kids who had trouble hearing and speaking. I remembered and made the connection for the first time in a couple of decades that I had known what I wanted to do professionally since childhood. And before I could say, "But," Steven said, "Same thing!" Indeed, it was the same thing. As a child, I only knew one kind of helping therapy, and that was it. But when I realized that my subconscious had hidden and at the same time followed that dormant calling, I woke up. All I knew was that every time I heard someone went to graduate school to study psychology, I felt a tinge of jealousy and self-doubt, like that could never be me. Still, this wasn't a great awakening, just one of the many that uncovered a childhood memory that had fallen out of view as I got further and further away from it.

Throughout the following years, I would come to discover how my inner voice had gone quiet and what I had forgotten along the way. That's what we do to get on with life: those unrealized parts of ourselves that we ignored for whatever reason will go dormant. Those unheard, undernourished and hidden parts of ourselves become the unseen barriers that keep us from trusting. Because, at the end of the day, no matter how much evidence, you must take the leap of trust that leads to faith. You don't jump because of what someone said or did or gave you – those things help build us like equipment in a gym – but it's because of our own awakening to self-love.

Here in the wild, mountainous terrain of self-love, we begin a journey to return to the unadulterated freedom of the animal that lives inside of us. This animal is like every grass, every stone, every bit of the earth on that mountain. It is intrinsically connected to its terrestrial and celestial elements, and has tacitly accepted what and how it lives. This acceptance comes through understanding that each moment and experience has been a lesson in how to live. How powerful it is to think of the self in this way, unfiltered by thoughts of yesterday or tomorrow! In other words, we use our senses to connect to our survival, rather than our senses using us to disconnect from that survival. For human beings, this is a process of accepting the order of our lives exactly as they have been, and using the impetus of those experiences to propel us to live with that wild-heart instinct. And as humans, we can take that instinct and elevate it to treat each moment as if it were life itself. In this re-awakening, the person that you thought you were remains, but the power of that animal comes through stronger, clearer and brighter.

This is the stuff self-worth is made of. The wild heart chooses to live from a clear, bright, strong place of faith, and to believe that everything we encounter and achieve is a story of self-realization, leading to unification of the self as we awaken our hearts.

When we awaken to acceptance of our lives, we can enter the process of forgiveness. Forgiveness of your internal heart is looking at that animal in you and releasing it back into the wild. Forgive the animal within for how you've held it back from running through the plains, the ridges, the peaks of that mountain. Forgive it for how you have allowed domestication to quiet its howl in the night. Give gratitude to this animal for staying deep within you throughout your life until you can finally release it back into the wild. Doing the latter is to love the inner self. This release is the faith, the trust that cannot be read or studied or acquired by knowing, only by loving.

Such loving gives rise to intuitive knowledge. Now, the window of intuition begins to broaden all the senses. This knowledge is among the most coveted of loves because only love is protected from the rational mind, and it is that release that reincorporates intuition. Intuition is that deep internal place of vibrational precision that leads us to close our eyes, enter our internal world, feel into our bodies, allow the flow of every sense within us to reveal the only truth there is – your truth. When this sense is nurtured, we begin to flourish in ways unimagined. Intuition is the child's orbit of gravitational connection. When we open ourselves up to that connection, our minds must release and allow the heart to feel and guide. Then, intuition becomes like a lightning force of energy that dispels the veils we created to protect ourselves from the world. One by one, each veil lifts, allowing more light, more love and more flow into your life.

This destiny requires commitment. It takes commitment to learn more about yourself, face yourself and stand up to and for yourself. This can be a painful process, but the acceptance of that pain is the liberation from it. That commitment helps to be supported by your openness to not having the answers or necessarily finding them, but to seeking truths within you that come through the gates of the heart. To read, study and explore across disciplines will ripen the energy of your path, but you must commit to this path knowing that it is a road of self-love. This path will help us to organize our thoughts and feelings so that we may learn to manage them.

This commitment is further supported by learning when and how to hold silence, and when and how to use our words. Our words are our gifts and our weapons. We must learn to use them in a way that is constructive and honest.

Be reminded that this is a journey that requires patience. This awakening is a rebirth of the self and requires time, understanding and compassion from the greatest source within you. Gather your mentors, your books and your tribe to support you, but always remember that you are the only one who is truly wise, truly the master of awakening your heart into the destiny that is already you.

CHAPTER 7

AMARANTHINE LOVE –
THE SEVENTH DESTINY

*Lucid emanation of dust
In the skies of the formless,
Gracing souls with love.
How beautiful each light,
Taking its place in infinity.*

The seventh destiny is amaranthine love. Here, we learn that love goes by many pseudonyms, but holds one vibration that is absolute, illuminating and unconditional, and transcends the time-space continuum. Amaranthine love brings the mind and heart into union with the soul as one. In this space we glimpse our own eternity. Here, we realize the agony of love is synonymous with love's ecstasy. Here, every practice, every thought, every study, every lesson, every feeling becomes a vital power of cosmic existence that returns us into shapeshifters of light.

What is required to attain amaranthine love is a life lived in service of love. Some of us will only catch a glimpse of this love in our lifetime, so we must stick to the practices that create peace and take us outside of our thought world. This is not about abandoning the mind, but more about coming into unity with the mind's purpose in our lives. The mind is a beautiful gift of surrealism, and, as such, we can create a reality that befits our destiny of love. We must learn to see the mind rather than be seen by the mind and, in turn, become a seer of the heart. We don't need to get out of our minds; we need to learn to love our minds so that we can love them as deeply as our essences. Here, loving the mind suggests a mastery of unconditional journeying through the depths of the narratives we live out. Whatever we have come to experience, our hearts are clear, and our job is to learn to bridge that clarity from heart to mind so that the mind becomes a companion.

This relationship of loving the mind begins with understanding that it is always a child, understanding and unconditional and, at the same time, stubborn and temperamental. The more the mind is soothed or actively stimulated, the more it fluctuates. Therefore, we must learn what things create negative stimulation that takes us far from a path of love; we must also uncover what creates positive stimulation that leads to a path of constructive and loving truths in our lives. The latter are the kinds of truths that help us to navigate into healthy relationships with ourselves and others. We must learn to understand what things make our minds impetuous and destructive. That way, we can hold compassion for it while allowing the heart to hold it in the boundaries of love that protect it from self-destruction. All of this can be cultivated through consciously learning values, beginning with the intention of doing no harm to oneself or others. This intention can help measure what the mind needs, whether it is safety, peace, joy or any other sensation. When we realize this, we are humbled to live lives of learning, wherein asking for help is normalized by the knowing that our soul journey is continuous, ongoing, purposeful and cosmically connected to everything and everyone.

In amaranthine love, you speak to the mind to foster a nurturing relationship: "I hear you, and I know this is your routine, thank you." You can also say, "I hear you. Unfortunately, I cannot follow you this time. I love you. I will not hurt you with my words, thoughts or actions. I will forgive you when you are lost. I will teach you when you are confused. Rely upon my heart as your greatest guide, and together we will travel this human journey through a space of love."

Ultimately, this distance travels to the centre of our humanity by bringing us home to the heart, where all is an undeniable tenderness, thanks to the gift of our mortality. We must embrace and learn to utilize all tangible senses throughout all our destinies so that we can attune to the instrument, releasing everything into cosmic silence that is beyond all logical scope. This scope is chartless, indeterminable, inexhaustible and illimitable, and so it enables the heart to unlock new senses yet to be named and understood.

In this destiny, we become conscious that the imprints we make take on a form, a life of their own. That is to say, how we live – whether it be by our thoughts or our actions, and even our inaction – makes tracks that impact every aspect of our reality. The significance of these tracks is deeply affected by this destiny because they come from a place of true love. These imprints change your destiny, the destiny of all those around you, and the destiny of those who come after you. That's because, when you make imprints based in love, you become a fierce gatekeeper and benevolent master of the universal heart.

Becoming a master of the universal heart occurs when you integrate all your love destinies. The master no longer solely sees from the self but from the heart, and in so doing, they hold compassion and understanding for every soul. The master is unbiased, and they break free of judgement and the shackles of mental polarity. Their view is not black or white or even grey, but instead shaded in crystalline love.

The amaranthine master is human, still able to err and experience the full gamut of their embodiment, but is also able to connect beneath the protection of this veil and see purely from heart to heart. This master holds loving compassion for all, seeing through their veils and into the radiance of each soul. The master sees all matter as if it were sacred, from ground to skies and everything in between. A wooden chair becomes the form it has taken, the service it provides, the craft, the crafter, the tree from whence it came, the mycelia beneath the trees connecting to the grid of all living things in the belly of the earth, and so on.

The insights of the amaranthine master are like waking up in the skies of fluidity where nature is yet to be discovered, thus allowing us to sit in the realization of our immutable essence. I cannot compete with great philosophies that attempt to define the undefinable essence of our being. I am referring to the essence of love that lives in each and every one of us. Did we invent love? Is it a human experience? Does it exist beyond our humanity? That is for you to determine. But love is the ultimate human being. That essence is unchangeable, that imprint is infinite, and love is ultimately unending.

This is how you love: by living from your heart. You love by remembering to live through the intention of loving yourself and others through every acceptance of who you are, which you broach with forgiveness, empathy, kindness and love. You learn to love each cell in your being as if it were its own universe. You learn to love every aspect of all that is imperfect so that you can see perfection.

Such love is freeing. It allows us to let go of all that we think we are and know, as we realize that it is an instinctual and instructional force of nature that we stray from, but it is always there, holding our connection to everything and everyone. From this vantage point, you realize that everything in your path is sacred in some way to your learning, growing, connecting and being. To love truly is to be human, whole and free. To become wholly human, we must allow this love to take us from the womb to the tomb, where we go back into the folds of nothingness while the trail of love we leave remains as the brightest light of our essence.

This perfect surrender allows us to step into dissolution, that place where we become fluid in our dimensionality, and our existence flows into the unknown, the possible and the probable. That dissolution is the freeing of the soul into the bliss of the great miracle of the universal heart.

For some, this return is the finding of the divine, the one, the ultimate who goes by many names. For some, there are angels, guides and spirits, too. This journey can be the light that dissolves all hearts into the mystical realms captured in poetry, philosophy, religion and texts both ancient and new. The amaranthine master knows they are all love.

CONCLUSION
EL DESTINO - DESTINY

Do not rage against death, injustice, war.
Rage for life.
Rage for justice.
Rage for peace and humanity.
Do not rage at fear of what was never yours or is yet to be.
Rage with awe at all that nature offers.
Rage for preservation of our earth.
Rage for compassion.
Rage for action and sacred activism.
Do not rage against your heart.
Rage with self-love.
Rage with life, with the floodgates of your compassionate soul.
Rage with inspiration that moves you to create change.
Rage with your innate ability to endure and thrive.
Rage with life.
Love is the door.

"El destino es el que baraja las cartas, pero nosotros somos los que jugamos."
I leave you with some final words that can only be spoken in my
mother tongue, the place where language emerged in my heart.
In English, this sentence says, "Destiny is the one that shuffles the
cards, but we are the ones that play them." As such, we must shuffle
the cards of love to fully embrace and embody the heartache and
rapture of love.

You are the amaranthine master, the lover of your destiny. Every day is an opportunity to step into that presence, no matter your age, your experience or lack thereof. Whatever absolution, validation, knowing or enlightenment you seek, it is within your heart. Be brave and walk through the gates of your destiny. Cry to your heart and ask it to guide you within.

You are a magnificent, loving soul. Your destiny of love is yours, and yours alone. Love in your way by allowing yourself to love wholly. Love with all of who you are in the full embrace of your heart. Surrender into love's mystic mystery so you can allow yourself to dissolve into its mastery. Create your own destinies and illuminate your path from the highest parts of your being. Whatever love destroys will give rise to a love greater than the one you knew. So, allow it to flow through the mist of your life and cultivate a fire so strong it will carry you into the depths of your soul.

Write your love story, tell your love story. Above all, live your love story. With love always, from my heart to yours.

The End.

THE SEVEN DESTINIES OF LOVE QUIZ

Below is a brief quiz you can take to discover which destinies of love are your strengths, as well as the areas in which you can continue to cultivate personal growth. The results are offered online. However, before taking the online version, I suggest exploring the answers to your questions here first, so you can get clarity about where you are and why. Beneath each question, you will find a space to answer and write your thoughts and feelings. When you are through, take the quiz a second time at www.theawakenedjourney.com and see if your answers change – this will guide you as you further explore your work.

One note: I do not personally score 100 per cent in all areas. Becoming the master of my love destinies is the work of my life. Thus, I must open my heart again and again into the light that is love. I hope you will do the same.

THE FIRST DESTINY

1. Which statement describes you best?

    A. I'm a thinker more than a lover.

    B. I'm a lover more than a thinker.

What about this statement fits? Is there more you'd like to explore and develop?

_____

_____

_____

_____
_____
_____

2. Which statement describes you best?
    A. I have awareness of my feelings.
    B. I have a hard time identifying my feelings.

What about this statement fits? Is there more you'd like to explore and develop?
_____
_____
_____
_____
_____
_____

3. Which statement describes you best?
    A. I know how to listen to my body.
    B. I don't really hear my body.

What about this statement fits? Is there more you'd like to explore and develop?
_____
_____
_____
_____
_____
_____

4. Which statement describes you best?
    A. I am comfortable with loving myself.
    B. I am uncomfortable with loving myself.

What about this statement fits? Is there more you'd like to explore and develop?

_____

_____

_____

_____

_____

_____

5. Which statement describes you best?
   A. I need to be right often.
   B. It's okay if others are right.

What about this statement fits? Is there more you'd like to explore and develop?

_____

_____

_____

_____

_____

_____

THE SECOND DESTINY

1. Which statement describes you best?
   A. I feel connected to the universe.
   B. I don't feel connected to the universe.

What about this statement fits? Is there more you'd like to explore and develop?

_____

_____

_____
_____
_____
_____

2. Which statement describes you best?

      A. I am aware of the lessons that life is trying to teach me.

      B. I am unaware of the lessons that life is trying to teach me.

What about this statement fits? Is there more you'd like to explore and develop?

_____
_____
_____
_____
_____
_____

3. Which statement describes you best?

      A. I am aware of the meanings of my life's lessons.

      B. I could use more insight to understand the lessons in my life.

What about this statement fits? Is there more you'd like to explore and develop?

_____
_____
_____
_____
_____
_____

4. Which statement describes you best?

      A. I am comfortable with the ebb and flow of feelings.

      B. I am uncomfortable with the ebb and flow of feelings.

What about this statement fits? Is there more you'd like to explore and develop?

_____

_____

_____

_____

_____

_____

5. Which statement describes you best?
    A. I am unsure of who I am.
    B. I am discovering who I am.

What about this statement fits? Is there more you'd like to explore and develop?

_____

_____

_____

_____

_____

_____

THE THIRD DESTINY

1. Which statement describes you best?
    A. I have healthy relationships with my family members.
    B. I have unhealthy relationships with my family members.

What about this statement fits? Is there more you'd like to explore and develop?

_____

_____

_____

_____

_____

_____

2. Which statement describes you best?

    A. I have a healthy relationship with myself.

    B. I have an unhealthy relationship with myself.

What about this statement fits? Is there more you'd like to explore and develop?

_____

_____

_____

_____

_____

3. Which statement describes you best?

    A. I feel connected in most of my relationships.

    B. I feel disconnected in most of my relationships.

What about this statement fits? Is there more you'd like to explore and develop?

_____

_____

_____

_____

_____

4. Which statement describes you best?

    A. I listen without reacting.

    B. I listen but I get reactive easily.

What about this statement fits? Is there more you'd like to explore and develop?

_____

_____

_____

_____

_____

_____

5. Which statement describes you best?
      A. I have a relationship with nature.
      B. I don't have a relationship with nature.

What about this statement fits? Is there more you'd like to explore and develop?

_____

_____

_____

_____

_____

_____

THE FOURTH DESTINY

1. Which statement describes you best?
      A. I am comfortable exploring my past.
      B. I am uncomfortable exploring my past.

What about this statement fits? Is there more you'd like to explore and develop?

_____

_____

_____

_____
_____
_____

2. Which statement describes you best?

    A. I feel connected to my ancestors.

    B. I feel disconnected from my ancestors.

What about this statement fits? Is there more you'd like to explore and develop?

_____
_____
_____
_____
_____
_____

3. Which statement describes you best?

    A. I have worked on reconciling my past.

    B. I have not reconciled my past.

What about this statement fits? Is there more you'd like to explore and develop?

_____
_____
_____
_____
_____
_____

4. Which statement describes you best?

    A. I have worked on my ancestral inheritance.

    B. I have not worked on my ancestral inheritance.

What about this statement fits? Is there more you'd like to explore and develop?

_____

_____

_____

_____

_____

_____

5. Which statement describes you best?
  A. I usually act from a place of love.
  B. I usually act from a place of fear.

What about this statement fits? Is there more you'd like to explore and develop?

_____

_____

_____

_____

_____

_____

THE FIFTH DESTINY

1. Which statement describes you best?
  A. My ego is my master.
  B. My ego is my helper.

What about this statement fits? Is there more you'd like to explore and develop?

_____

_____

_____

2. Which statement describes you best?

      A. I have undertaken my own learning to enhance my self-development.

      B. I have not learned much about self- development.

What about this statement fits? Is there more you'd like to explore and develop?

_____

_____

_____

_____

_____

_____

3. Which statement describes you best?

      A. I am interested in exploring my soul's purpose through the way I live.

      B. I am unclear of what my soul's purpose is.

What about this statement fits? Is there more you'd like to explore and develop?

_____

_____

_____

_____

_____

4. Which statement describes you best?

      A. I am comfortable with the inexplicable elements of life.

B. I am uncomfortable with the inexplicable elements of life.

What about this statement fits? Is there more you'd like to explore and develop?

_____

_____

_____

_____

_____

_____

5. Which statement describes you best?
      A. I trust my intuition.
      B. I don't trust my intuition.

What about this statement fits? Is there more you'd like to explore and develop?

_____

_____

_____

_____

_____

_____

THE SIXTH DESTINY

1. Which statement describes you best?
      A. I am in the process of awakening spiritually.
      B. I don't feel spiritually awakened.

What about this statement fits? Is there more you'd like to explore and develop?

_____

_____

_____

_____

_____

_____

2. Which statement describes you best?

    A. I mostly live in the present moment.

    B. I mostly live in the past or future.

What about this statement fits? Is there more you'd like to explore and develop?

_____

_____

_____

_____

_____

3. Which statement describes you best?

    A. I have a balanced memory of both positive and negative experiences in my life.

    B. I have an imbalanced memory with more positive or negative experiences in my life.

What about this statement fits? Is there more you'd like to explore and develop?

_____

_____

_____

_____

_____

4. Which statement describes you best?

    A. I have reconciled who I was taught to be in comparison to who I want to be, and I have instead developed my own sense of self.

    B. I have not reconciled who I was taught to be in comparison with who I want to be, and I don't have a secure sense of self.

What about this statement fits? Is there more you'd like to explore and develop?

_____

_____

_____

_____

_____

_____

5. Which statement describes you best?

    A. I have worked on forgiveness for myself and others.

    B. I have not worked on forgiveness for myself and others.

What about this statement fits? Is there more you'd like to explore and develop?

_____

_____

_____

_____

_____

_____

THE SEVENTH DESTINY

1. Which statement describes you best?

    A. I feel I can truly love unconditionally.

B. I feel I love with conditions.

What about this statement fits? Is there more you'd like to explore and develop?

_____

_____

_____

_____

_____

_____

2. Which statement describes you best?
    A. I am living a life in service of love.
    B. I am living a life that could be more in service of love.

What about this statement fits? Is there more you'd like to explore and develop?

_____

_____

_____

_____

_____

_____

3. Which statement describes you best?
    A. I love my thoughts.
    B. I don't love my thoughts.

What about this statement fits? Is there more you'd like to explore and develop?

_____

_____

_____

_____

_____

_____

4. Which statement describes you best?

     A. I am comfortable with the concept of death.

     B. I am uncomfortable with the concept of death.

What about this statement fits? Is there more you'd like to explore and develop?

_____

_____

_____

_____

_____

_____

5. Which statement describes you best?

     A. I have an inner sense of peace and love.

     B. I am still working on my inner sense of peace and love.

What about this statement fits? Is there more you'd like to explore and develop?

_____

_____

_____

_____

_____

_____

YOUR LOVE DESTINY JOURNAL

This book is intended to be a process, so it may require that
you reference it again throughout different stages of your life. I
encourage you to journal and perhaps reflect on some of the lessons
you have learned, questions that have arisen and feelings that have
surfaced, so that you may look back on them each time you work
through aspects of a different love destiny. At the same time, I have
created a space for you to write the most important love destiny –
your destiny as you envision it filled with love. Jot notes, missives and
love letters, and remember it is all in service of love.

_____

_____

_____

_____

_____

_____

_____

_____

_____

_____

_____

_____

_____

_____

_____

_____

_____

_____

MY LOVE DESTINY: _____

_____

_____

_____

_____

_____

_____

_____

_____

_____

_____

_____

_____

_____

_____

_____

_____

_____

_____

_____

_____

_____

_____

_____

_____

_____

_____

_____

_____

_____

_____

_____

_____

_____

_____

ENDORSEMENTS

This book is heaven sent, as if it was called forth by the yearning of our time. Claudia de Llano's words are poetically beautiful, like a calm, reassuring presence, reminding us that our purpose, our reason for being, always comes back to the heart.

It's an invitation to reconnect to our loving essence as a crucial step in evolution and offers a new perspective on emotions, awakening us to the essential truth – which many of us have long forgotten – that we are inseparable from love.

– Jacinta Tynan, journalist and author of *The Single Mother's Social Club*, www.jacintatynan.com

It's with the deepest gratitude that I'm able to share my reaction to reading *The Seven Destinies of Love* by Claudia De Llano.

There are a handful of people that I credit with having the greatest impact on my approach to life, both from a professional and a personal perspective. Claudia is at the very top of that list. Since that day I met her, when she served as my supervisor in a stress-filled and high-expectation work environment, she has been a mentor... a guiding light in how to tackle the trials of life with the intention of harnessing both the good and the bad for personal growth.

Claudia has lived in the trenches of adversity and challenge... and she has honed a masterful approach to understanding how compassion, empathy and love can serve as a powerful tool in unlocking the treasures that life holds for each and every one of us.

I'm thrilled to see her put these lessons down in writing, and I believe that countless individuals can use this exceptional book as a totem for their own blossoming into the space of self-realization. This book is a beautiful masterclass in loving oneself.

– Brian Gott, Chief Innovation Officer for The Entertainment Industry Foundation and former publisher for *Variety*

Claudia de Llano's heartwarming book *The Seven Destinies of Love* offers readers powerful, illuminating guidance for navigating the lifelong journey of love. With her groundbreaking seven-step paradigm, Claudia brings readers face to face with the truth of love's power to help us nurture fulfillment, joy and deeply satisfying relationships. The reader's journey is supported with tools including a quiz and space for reflective journaling. If you're craving a gentle journey into the soulful world of genuine love, *The Seven Destinies* is a brilliant treasure.

– Carla Marie Manly, Ph.D., clinical psychologist and award-winning author

Love truly is the essence of who we are individually and collectively, but it is often forgotten in a world of deadlines, expectations and questions about our own worth. Claudia has beautifully invited us to find our way back to ourselves: love of who we are in our purist form, love of those whose shoulders we stand on, love for those around us, love for the earth that allows us to inhabit its natural beauty and love for those yet to come. Claudia reminds us to live with an open heart because healing happens in moments woven together across a lifetime.

– Joanne Weingarten, Psy.D., psychologist and grief expert

ABOUT THE AUTHOR

Claudia de Llano, M.A., is a Marriage and Family Therapist, speaker, yoga instructor and meditation guide. She facilitates the awakening of inner harmony and conscious being.

A healer of the heart, she helps people transcend from stories of pain and challenge to lead lives of love and fulfilment. She is interested in helping people define who they are and find their footing on the paths they want to follow. Well versed in systemic and strength-based psychological theories, she has helped individuals in clinical and business settings move through partnership, career growth and personal development, among other life challenges.

Claudia's expertise is embedded in deep multicultural understanding and mind-body-spirit integration through a synthesis of psychological and alternative therapies. She believes that each individual is capable of tapping into their true nature. Her passion inspires others to discover their own psychology and unique life paths.

Claudia began her career in entertainment publicity and corporate communications. She holds a master's degree in psychology with a specialization in multicultural training. She has held faculty positions at Phillips Graduate University and National University. Claudia is a certified yoga, meditation and reiki practitioner. Her recent corporate engagements have covered topics including resilience, well-being, stress reduction, mindfulness and mental health in the workplace.

Claudia has been living abroad throughout Asia-Pacific with her husband and daughter for the last nine years. You can find her online at www.theawakenedjourney.com.

ACKNOWLEDGEMENTS

With love and gratitude from deep within my heart to my father Alberto de Llano for a life of unconditional love. To my beautiful daughter Juliana for expanding my heart, my vision and my life. To the bedrock of my heart, my husband Mark, who is the co-creator of my dreams, this is for you. To my family – Bertha, Aymara and Gerardo – my constants, my blessings, I love you. To Debbie and Joe, all my love for how you have made me a part of your family.

A profound thanks to Dr Jose Luis Flores, who opened the floodgates of Bowenian therapy and forever led me down a path of self-differentiation. To my teachers and colleagues who helped build and support my path. To Deborah Buttitta, thank you for believing in me. To Veda Sande for the illuminating presence you have been in my life. To Fereshteh Mazdyazni for being a voice of guidance that is always with me. To Lucy Proud, the mirror of my awakening, the spiritual sister of my soul and the light of an eternal friendship. To Stephanie Johnson for a lifetime sisterhood and unconditional love. To Vanessa Lynn Payne, my special one, this could not have happened without you; thank you for all your work and support. To Angela Trigger for your beautiful light. To Laurie Mucha for your friendship, and for leading me down a path that would forever shape my life. To Dr Joanne Weingarten for your spirit and friendship. To Courtney Kretchman for always smiling brightly into my heart. To Trina O'Hara for being a friend and witness to my process. To Brian Gott for your magnanimous heart and contribution to this book. To T'Keyah Crystal Keymáh, who speaks the language of crystalline love. To Ernest Fung for generously giving to this vision. To Enoch Li with gratitude for encouraging the deadline and the work you do to make a difference. To Renny Ruiz for interpreting my story through your art. To Ram Dass, who I never met, but who truly knew my heart.

Lastly, to my students and my clients who have shared their lives with me. Thank you for allowing me to be a part of your journey. It is you who inspire me, motivate me and awaken me to a life in service of love.

ABOUT CHERISH EDITIONS

Cherish Editions is a bespoke self-publishing service for authors of mental health, well-being and inspirational books.

As a division of Trigger Publishing, the UK's leading independent mental health and well-being publisher, we are experienced in creating and selling positive, responsible, important and inspirational books, which work to de-stigmatize the issues around mental health and improve the mental health and well-being of those who read our titles.

Founded by Adam Shaw, a mental health advocate, author and philanthropist, and leading psychologist Lauren Callaghan, Cherish Editions aims to publish books that provide advice, support and inspiration. We nurture our authors so that their stories can unfurl on the page, helping them to share their uplifting and moving stories.

Cherish Editions is unique in that a percentage of the profits from the sale of our books goes directly to leading mental health charity Shawmind, to deliver its vision to provide support for those experiencing mental ill health.

Find out more about Cherish Editions by visiting cherisheditions.com or joining us on:

    Twitter @cherisheditions
    Facebook @cherisheditions
    Instagram @cherisheditions

Cherish
EDITIONS

ABOUT SHAWMIND

A proportion of profits from the sale of all Trigger books go to their sister charity, Shawmind, also founded by Adam Shaw and Lauren Callaghan. The charity aims to ensure that everyone has access to mental health resources whenever they need them.

Find out more about the work Shawmind do by visiting shawmind.org or joining them on:

Twitter @Shawmind_
Facebook @ShawmindUK
Instagram @Shawmind_

Your Local Mental Health & Wellbeing Charity